WORLD IN DANGER

EARTH

Steve Pollock
Illustrated by Peter Wingham

Belitha Press

First published in Great Britain in 1991 by
Belitha Press Limited
31 Newington Green, London N16 9PU

Editor: Neil Champion

ISBN 1-85561-060-4 (Hardback)
ISBN 1-85561-092-2 (Paperback)

Reprinted 1991, 1992
Printed in Hong Kong for Imago

Contents

The land around us

From tropical forest, to deserts, to deep canyons in the ground, the Earth has an amazing variety of landscapes. How does it happen? It's caused by the land itself moving, by the weather, by animals and plants and sometimes by people.

The Grand Canyon in the USA was carved out of rock by the force of a river gouging through the land. Deserts are found where hardly any rain falls. **Tropical forests** only grow where there is lots of rain and warmth.

When people started growing crops they changed the appearance of the land. In parts of Europe the land was parcelled up in fields. Fences and hedges are now part of our landscape.

People can never change the landscape like the sudden force of a volcano or earthquake can. Movement deep inside the Earth makes the ground shift, shake and twist. Boiling rock called **lava** comes gushing from deep inside the Earth and spills out of a volcano.

Volcano

Earthquake

Most changes to the Earth are slower and take longer. Rivers, frost, ice, the wind all work together to shape the land gradually. It has taken millions of years and it is still going on even today. Any place we see today will be very different a million years from now.

Changing landscapes

Before people appeared on Earth much of the land would have been covered in thick forest. People cut the forest down and grew crops on the soil. They built villages and roads. They dug stones out of the ground to make their buildings. These changes took place slowly at first. This picture shows what a landscape may have looked like about 250 years ago. The changes people have made are already very obvious.

Today the same landscape looks like this. What was once a village is now a city. What was once a track is now a highway. There are industries making goods. People who work in the industries need houses to live in. The food they eat no longer comes from the fields nearby, but from a long way away. So the landscape changes and with these changes come dangers to the land caused by modern people's needs.

Look carefully at these pictures. What differences can you see between them? Where do you think the danger to the land might be?

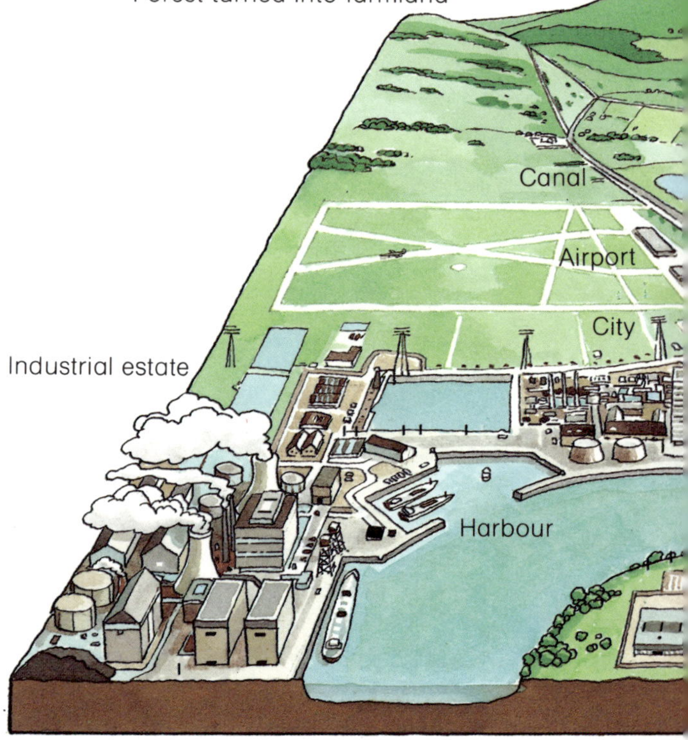

A landscape
250 years ago

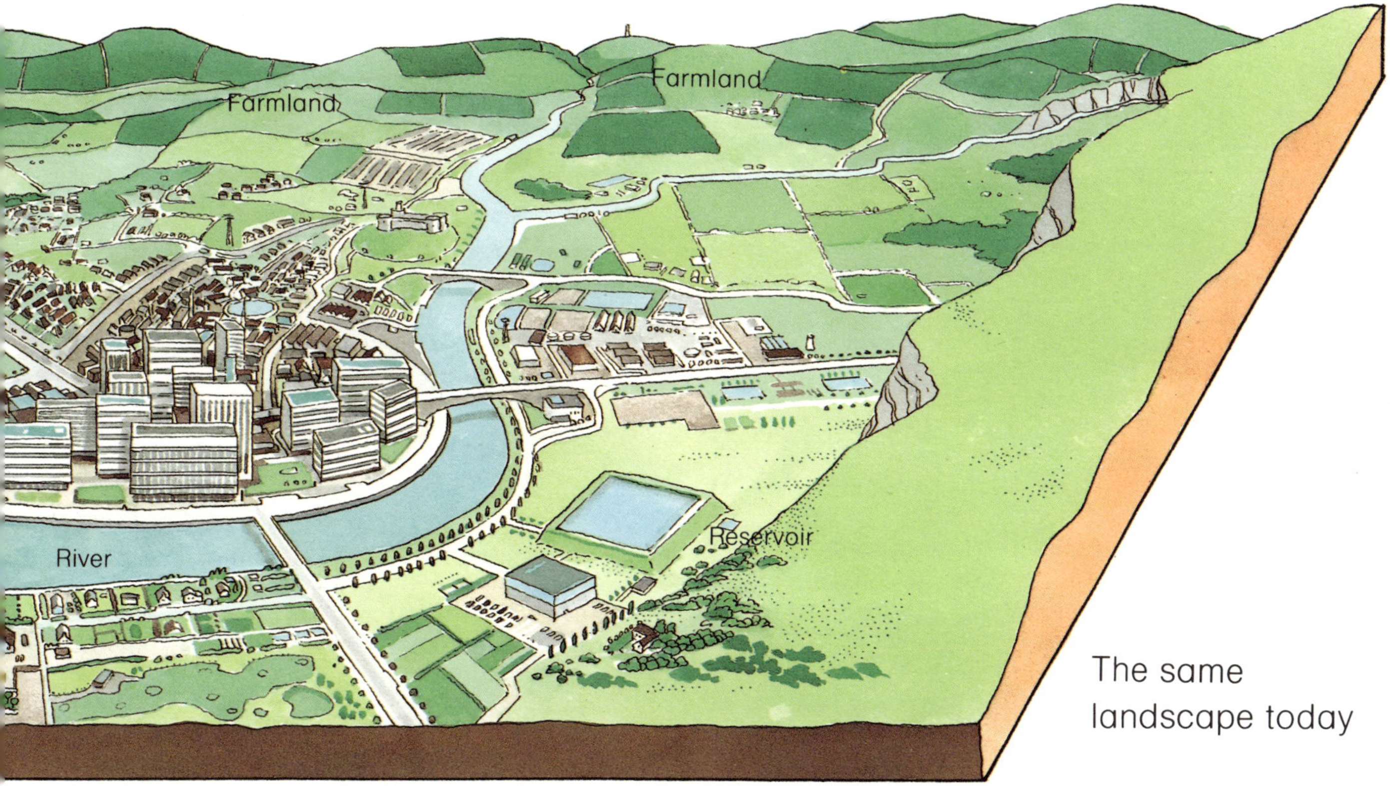

The same
landscape today

Making soil

Soil is made from tiny pieces of rock and rotted pieces of dead leaves and other once-living things. The rock is broken into tiny pieces by rain, cracked by the heat of the sun and split by the freezing cold frost and ice. Plants grow in the cracks. Bits of dead plants and rock mix together to make soil.

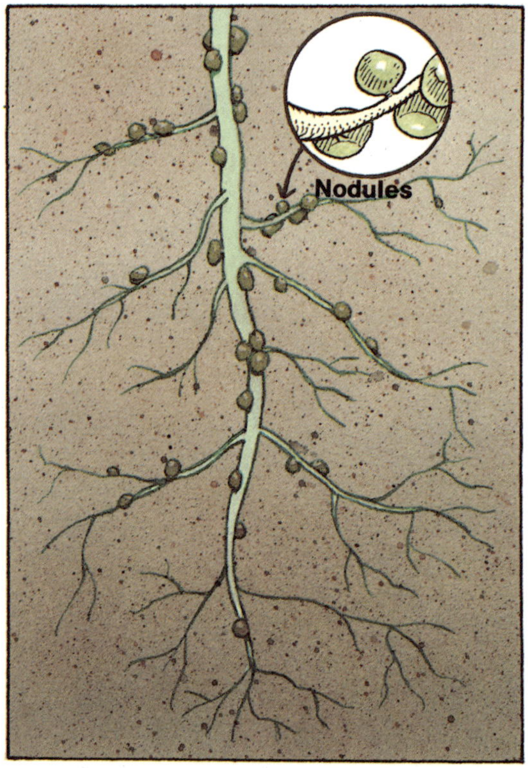

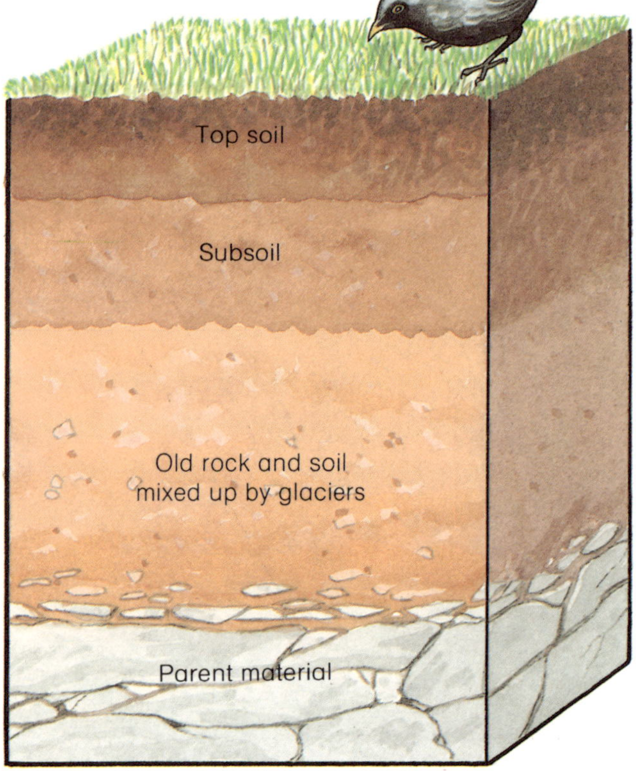

Soil gathers over millions of years. It makes different layers – the top soil, sub-soil and parent rock. Some soils are better than others for growing plants. Certain kinds of plants have special lumps on their roots (nodules). These can turn **nitrogen gas** from the air into **chemicals** that help plants to grow. Peas, clover and lupins do this.

Under the soil live thousands of tiny animals which cannot be seen without a magnifying glass. But there are bigger animals like worms and moles which make homes in the soil. Soil is important for supporting all life on land.

Without it no plants could grow and there would be nothing for animals to eat. The different animals and plants which live in the soil help keep it healthy.

One kind of soil is made from dead plant material that has not rotted down completely. This is called peat. It is dug up and sold for gardening and is in danger because of this.

Peat digging
Peat is soil material made from plants in swamps and bogs. It is used by gardeners and for burning as fuel.

Soil cycles

A group of small animals and plants help to break down nature's rubbish into smaller parts. These are the decomposers. Animals such as woodlice, millipedes and beetles are decomposers. They feed on dung, the bodies of dead animals and the dead parts of plants. Many live in or on the soil. Mushrooms rot down materials such as wood. They have a web of microscopic strands called **hyphae.** **Microscopic bacteria** help to decompose nature's waste into chemicals. All this waste can then be re-used for growing new life.

Soil cycles

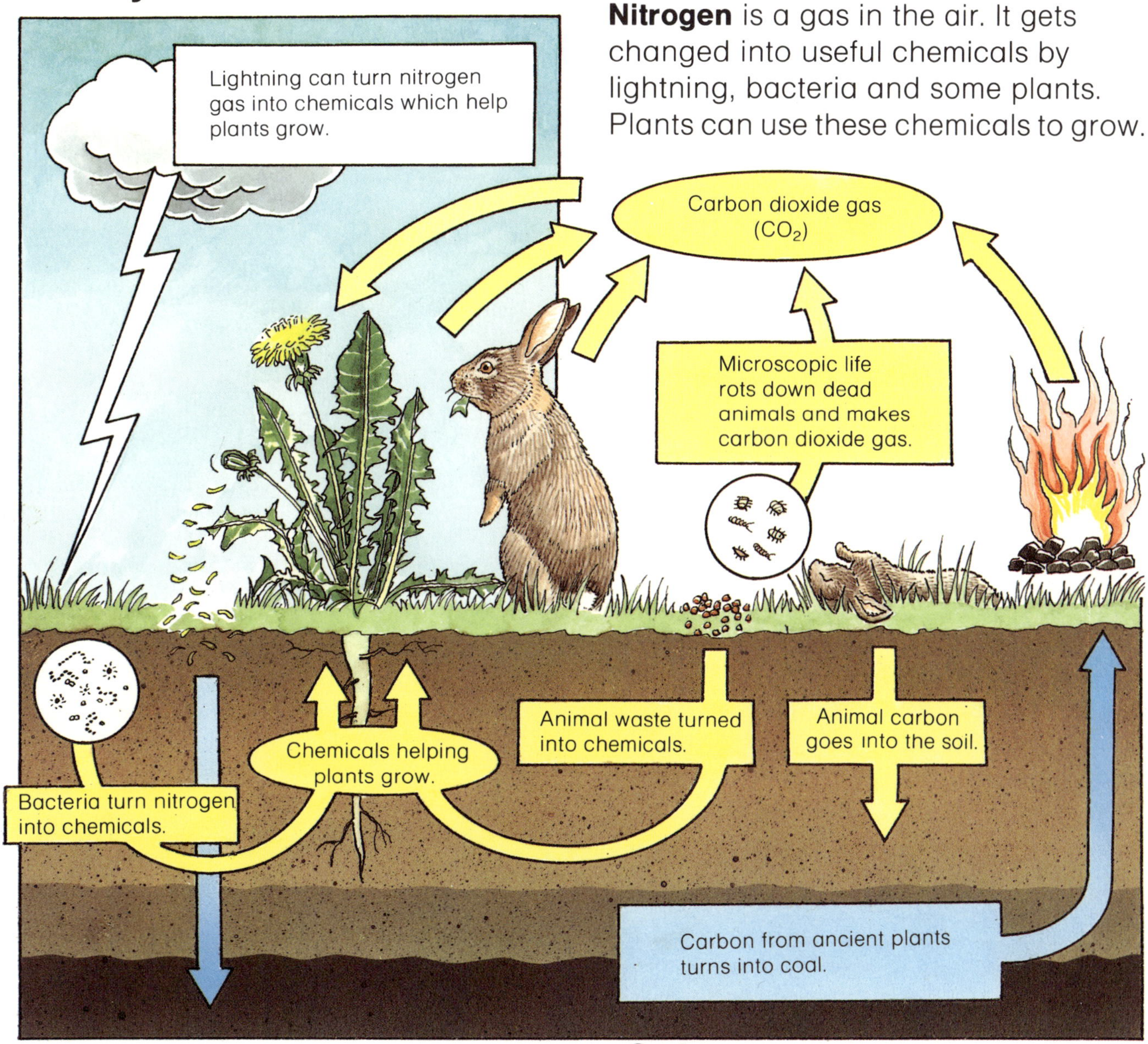

Nitrogen

Nitrogen is a gas in the air. It gets changed into useful chemicals by lightning, bacteria and some plants. Plants can use these chemicals to grow.

The soil plays a very important part in recycling the world's natural supply of chemicals. In particular two gases are important to all life. These are nitrogen and **carbon dioxide**.

Carbon

All living things have carbon in them. Carbon is returned to the soil by **decomposers** and to the air as carbon dioxide. Plants re-use this carbon to grow. Nothing is wasted in nature.

Caring for the soil

In some countries there is little good, flat land. People have to grow their crops on hillsides. Heavy rains can easily wash the soil away. The hillsides are **terraced** to hold onto the soil.

In other countries the heavy rains are used for growing crops such as rice. Rice is planted under water in these flooded paddy fields. The water changes the soil making it just right for rice growing. Some farmers in Europe use a natural or **organic** system for growing crops. They use animals such as pigs to eat the remains of the old crop. The pigs add their dung. This **fertilizes** the soil. They plant clover which helps the soil too. They can then grow a crop without using bags of chemical fertilizers.

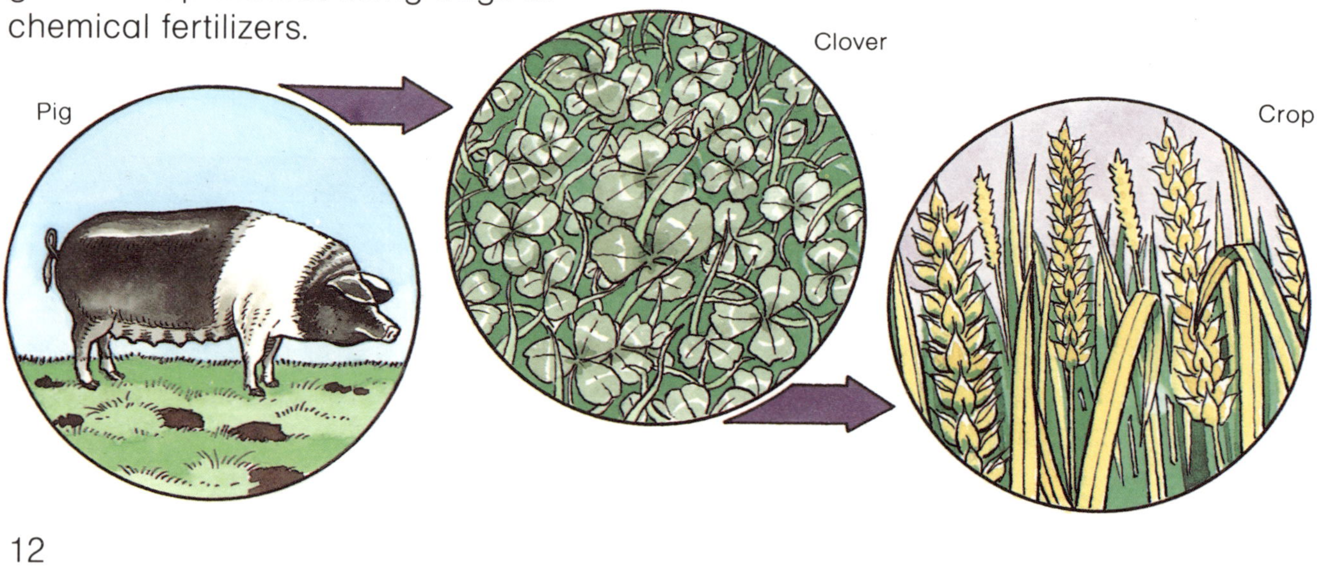

People living in tropical forests find ways to live off the land. They clear a patch of ground by cutting down the trees and burning them. This makes the soil rich for two or three years. The people can grow their crops in the soil helped by the ash of the burnt trees. They then move on to clear another patch of forest. In the meantime the patch of cleared forest grows back. For hundreds of years tribal people have lived this way using the soil. Today, more and more people without any work are moving from the towns and cities to live in the forest. This puts the land in great danger because there are just too many people and not enough forest.

The forest cannot grow back so fast if it is always being cut down. Also the forest is at risk from being burnt down. It also puts the tribal people who live there in danger, too.

Losing the soil

On the **prairies** of North America the grass is turned over to growing wheat today. **Combine harvesters** pass over the open prairies collecting tonnes and tonnes of wheat. Much of it feeds other parts of the world, not just North America.

There was a time in the 1930s when bad farming and dry weather turned part of the prairies into a **dust bowl**. The farmers could grow nothing. Farmers now plant trees to stop the wind blowing soil away. But in other countries hedges have been removed, allowing the wind to blow soil away. Good soil is still being blown away even today.

The River Nile . . . floods onto the land . . . leaving its rich mud.

The ancient Egyptians used the flooding of the River Nile to fertilize their land. Every winter mud from the river collected on the banks. Channels were made to take the water and mud out on to the land. The mud made the ground so fertile that the ancient Egyptians could grow enough food to feed thousands of people.

Electricity from the Aswan Dam gave people modern things like TVs.

In the 1960s the Aswan Dam was built. It gave electricity to many Egyptians. But the dam stopped the mud of the River Nile from fertilizing the land. Today Egyptians use fertilizer made in factories to grow their crops.

From soil to desert

In some of the world's very hot continents, such as Africa, much of the good land is owned by only a few people. A lot of it is used to grow crops to sell to other countries, not to feed the people living there. This forces people to farm poor land. When a lot of people's cattle **graze** on poor land it becomes useless.

This has been made worse by other countries giving money for extra wells and medicine for the cattle. More cattle are kept on this poor land, so nothing can grow. It only takes a few dry years and the people's cattle begin to die. Eventually the people suffer as they too have nothing to eat.

Money from rich countries . . .

. . . to build wells

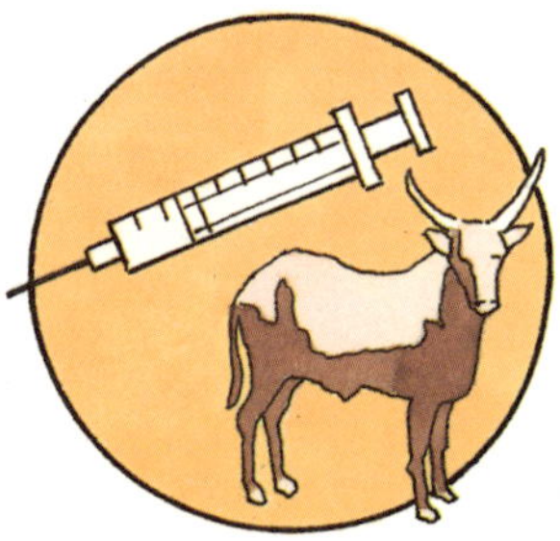

. . . to buy medicine for animals.

Trees cut down

Rain washes soil away

Floods destroy villages

People move away

In mountainous countries such as Nepal, people are forced to cut down trees for firewood, just to cook a meal and stay warm. Without the trees, the soil washes away in the heavy monsoon rains. Villages disappear under mud or are flooded out. People then have to move away and find other places to live.

In many hot countries extra water is put on the land to grow crops. This is called **irrigation**. In Australia a lot of land has become useless because it has become salty. That's because the extra water **dissolves** deep in the soil. The heat draws the water out of the ground taking the salts with it to the surface. When the salts reach the surface they ruin the soil.

Salts deep in the ground move slowly to the surface, spoiling the top soil.

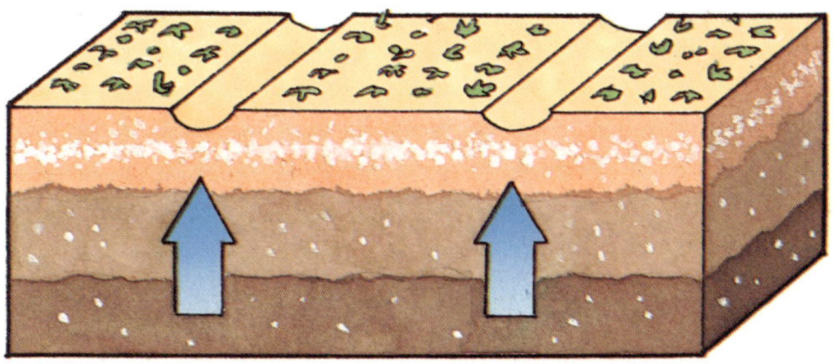

Too much of a good thing?

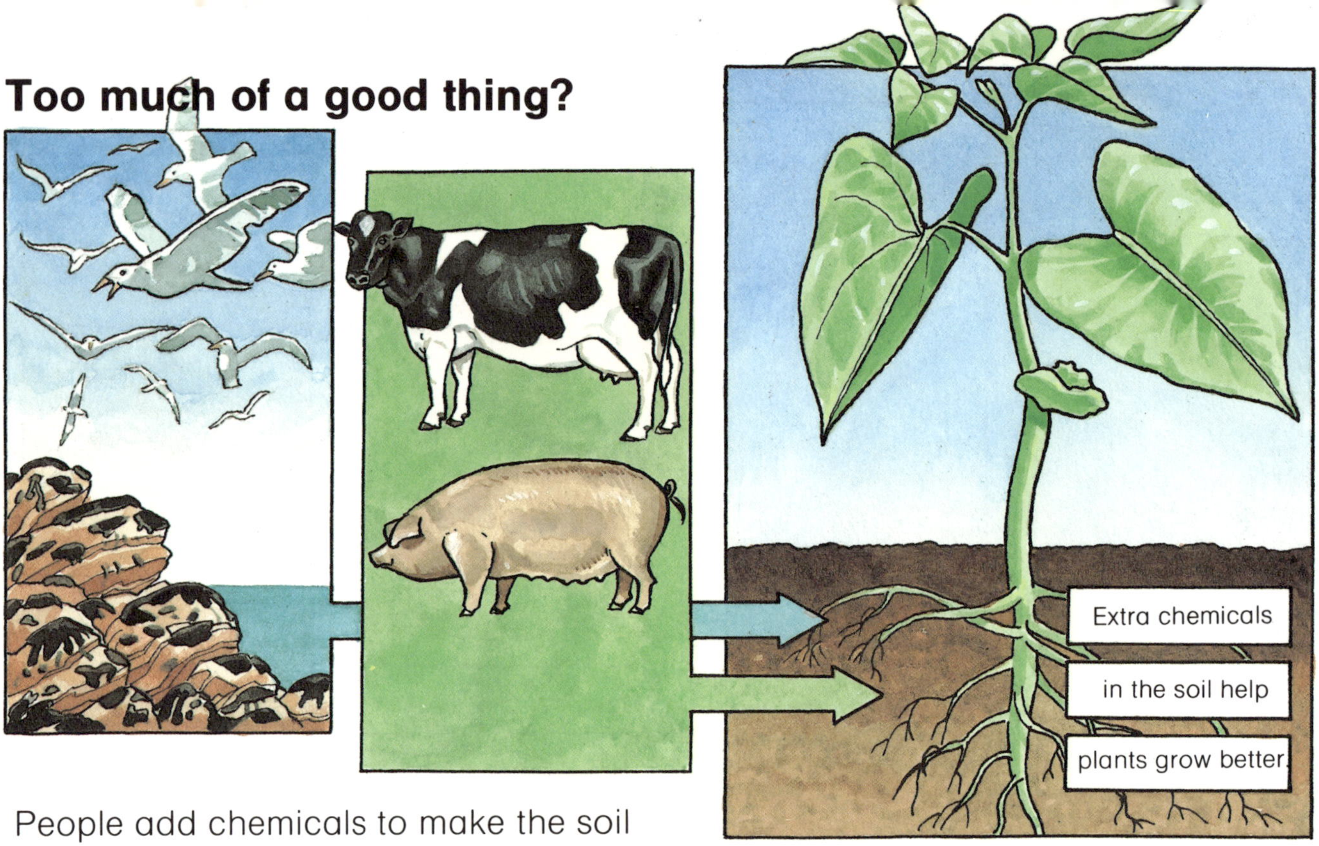

People add chemicals to make the soil grow more crops. This is called fertilizing the soil. For a long time farmers used the dung of animals such as pigs and cows to fertilize the soil. Not so long ago the droppings of sea birds, called **guano,** were dug up and used as a fertilizer. This was sent all over the world. These fertilizers are natural fertilizers.

Today all over the world fertilizers are made in factories. These are artificial fertilizers. Farmers then put them on the land themselves. Too much fertilizer can be dangerous because it can get into drinking water.

Much more dangerous to the land are chemicals called **pesticides**. Pesticides are poisonous chemicals. They are used for killing animals which eat the farmer's crops. They work well killing off many pests. This means there is more food for people and less for the pests. Problems arise when other animals eat the crops.

In their turn they are eaten by other animals. This is called a food chain. The animal at the top of the food chain will have eaten so much that it may become sick and die. People are at the top of the food chains. Are we eating too much of this pesticide? We don't really know.

A Food Chain

Precious gifts

Much of today's modern industry and people's day to day lives can run only because of the land's natural materials. These are coal, oil and gas. Without them much of modern daily life would come to a complete stand still.

Coal is made from plants which were alive millions of years ago. Changes in the land turned the carbon in the plants to coal. This took millions of years to happen. Oil is made from the bodies of tiny animals which lived in the sea millions of years ago. Over time, rocks pressed down on the dead animals turning them into oil. When oil is formed like this gas is also made.

There is a danger that the world's supply of oil, gas and coal will one day be used up. However, some of the world's natural resources can never be exhausted. There will always be wind.

Windmills can use this supply of energy. Another kind of energy is geothermal energy. This is heat from rocks deep in the ground. In some parts of the world water is pumped down to these rocks turning it into hot water or steam, which is pumped back up to be used for heating houses and making things work.

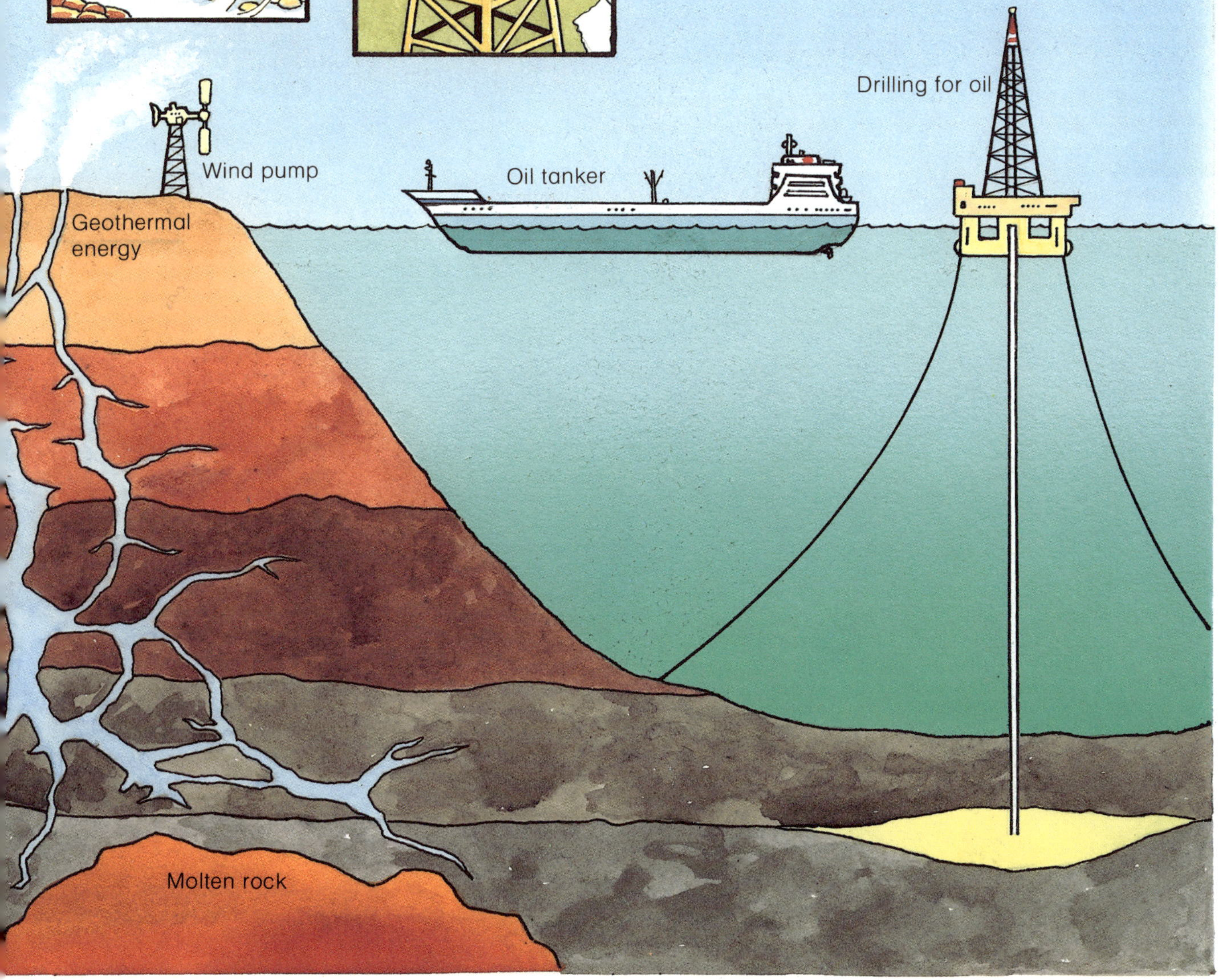

Holes in the ground

The land has always provided people with the materials they need. Marble dug from quarries has been used since early times for building. Today ores taken from the ground are used to make modern technology. Digging up these valuable materials can damage the land. It spoils the landscape.

In some countries the land is used to store the rubbish from people's houses. The rubbish is put in huge holes in the ground. These holes are called land-fill sites. When they are full they may be covered over with soil and planted with trees.

In some places the ugly landscape made by people has been turned back into something which looks more natural. Gravel pits have been allowed to fill with water. Trees and bushes have been planted around the pits. After a few years the landscape has changed and appears more natural.

Very dangerous waste is placed in special chambers under ground. With all this waste there is a risk that one day it might escape and cause pollution. So even the land underground is in danger.

Wasteland becomes . . .

a dry ski-slope

Solving problems

There are ways to stop land turning to desert. The diagram shows what can be done to hold on to the soil which washes or blows away.

There are ways to make sure land is kept healthy for crop growing. In Sri Lanka a buddhist monk was sent to a village. He saw villagers cutting down trees for building and firewood. He knew there would be no more trees left.

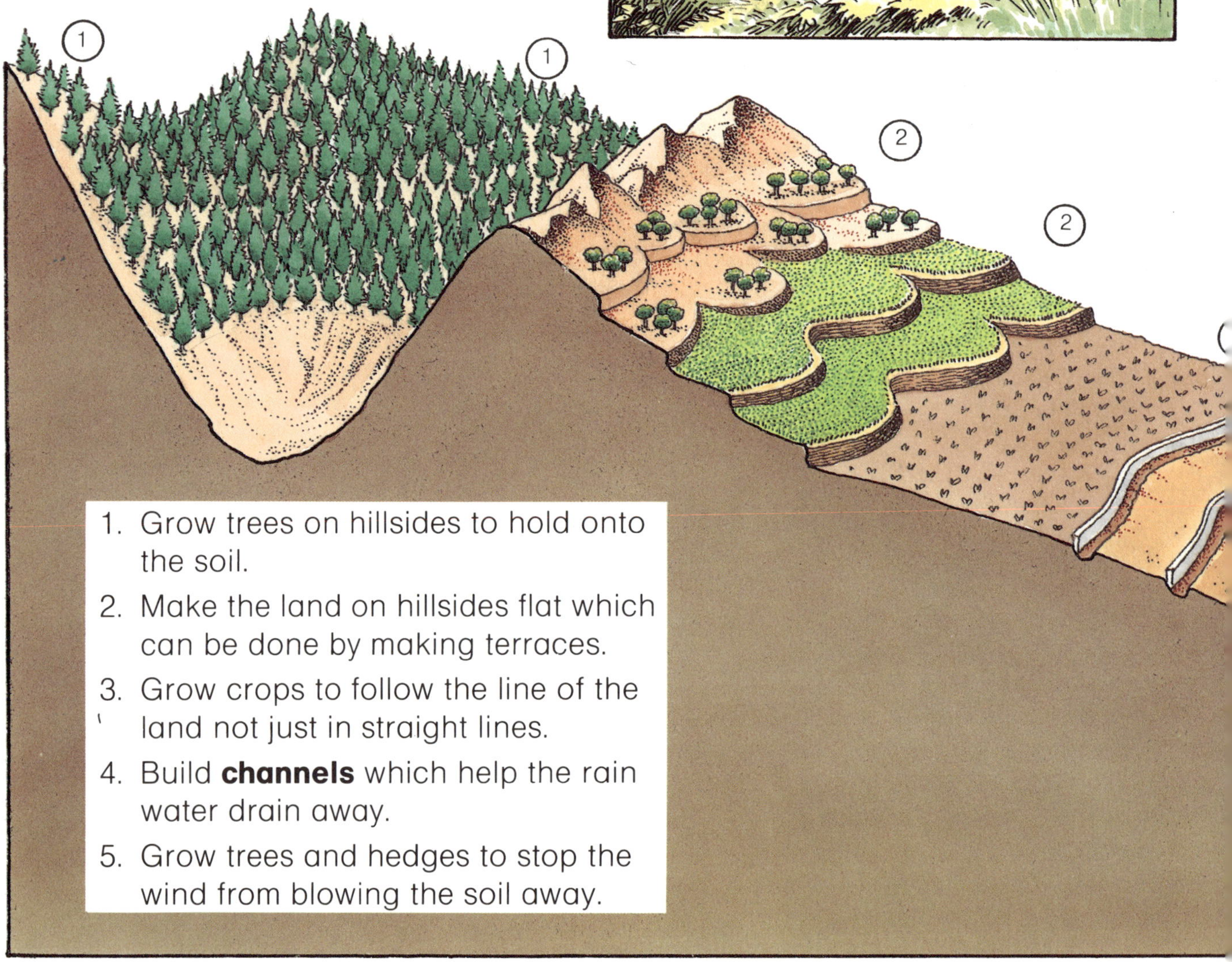

1. Grow trees on hillsides to hold onto the soil.
2. Make the land on hillsides flat which can be done by making terraces.
3. Grow crops to follow the line of the land not just in straight lines.
4. Build **channels** which help the rain water drain away.
5. Grow trees and hedges to stop the wind from blowing the soil away.

In the end the villagers would have to move away. Like many people in the world they did not own their land.

So the monk suggested the Government give each family two acres of land. They planted an acre to grow a crop to sell and earn money, half an acre for trees to protect the soil and the rest for growing food for the family.

The monk planted young trees. The young people of the village looked after them. By doing this they would always know the value of trees for the land. The village could now look forward to a much brighter future. The monk had helped them own their land and showed them ways to make sure it stayed in good health for a long, long time.

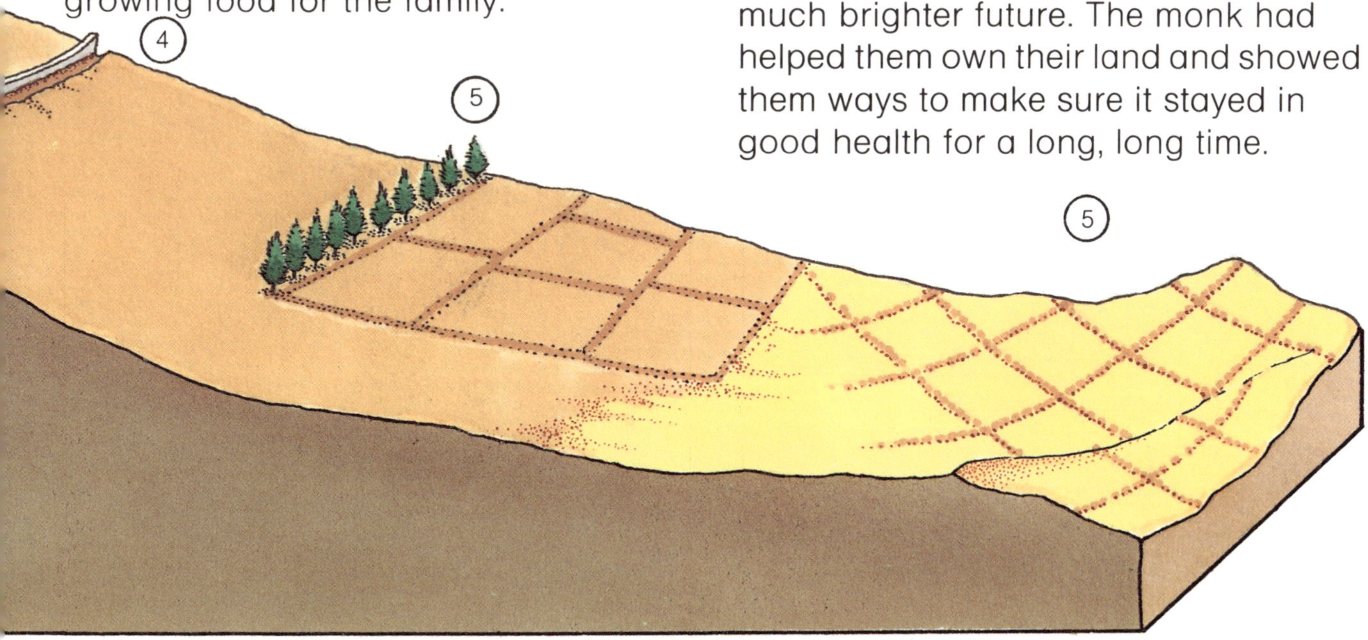

Discovering soil

To find out what the soil is like in your area empty some onto a piece of newspaper. What can you find? Does it feel very crumbly? Is it wet? Does it clump together or spread out easily? Are there many leaves and bits of plant material in it? What about animals living in it like worms? To find out more about soils look at the fact file on pages 28 and 29.

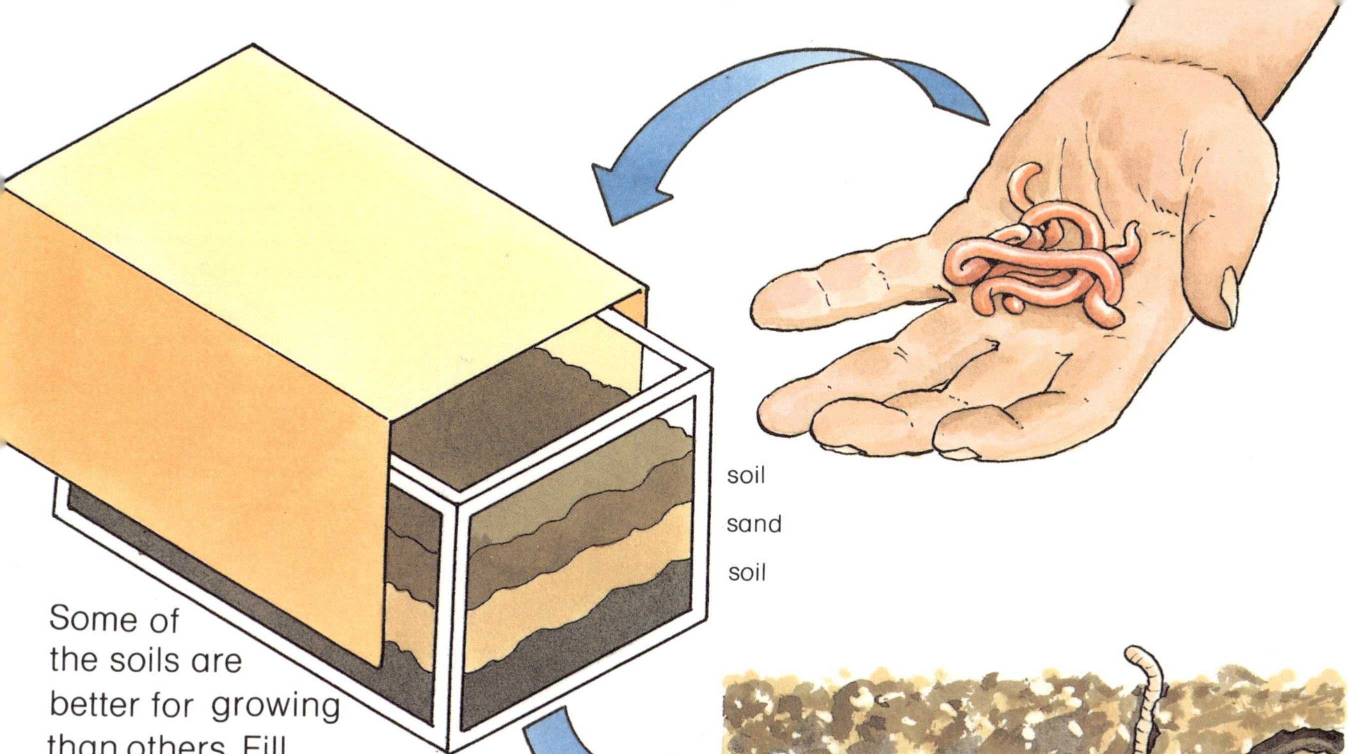

Some of the soils are better for growing than others. Fill three plant pots with different soils. One with an ordinary soil, one with clay and the other with sand. Plant seeds from the same packet and water them regularly. How do they grow? Which soil is best for the plants to grow in?

You may have found worms in your soil. Worms are important for keeping the soil healthy. To find out what they do, half fill a glass container such as a fish tank with soil. Place a layer of sand on top of the soil and put another layer of soil on top of the sand. Add a few worms and cover the tank with paper. Keep the soil moist. After a few days what has happened to the layer of sand? Can you see many worm holes through the glass?

Land fact file

Soil

The soil is likely to be sandy and well drained when the ground underneath is sandy. Sandy soils are quite light and water drains through them quickly. Clay soils feel heavy and damp because they hold onto water. Some soils will be much darker than others because there is more plant material, like dead leaves, in it. This plant material is called humus.

The best soil for growing plants is called a loam. This is a mixture of clay, sand and humus. The clay gives the soil important minerals for plant growth. The sand keeps the soil loose and well drained. The humus is the material from decayed plants which gives the plant the chemicals it needs to grow.

Losing soil

It has been worked out that it takes between 300-1,000 years to create an inch of soil, depending on the kind of rock it comes from and the climate. American farmers are losing an inch of soil every sixteen years because of the way they farm. So it will not be long before the soil goes completely as it is being worn away much quicker than it's being made.

Rubbish!

Country	*Annual domestic waste (tonnes)*	*Equivalent per person (kgs)*
USA	200,000,000	875
Japan	40,225,000	344
Great Britain	15,816,000	282
New Zealand	1,528,000	488

This is how much household rubbish is collected every year in four countries. Much of it is thrown into holes in the ground where there is a risk of pollution.

Disaster in Nepal
Each year one quarter of a million tonnes of topsoil are washed down from the treeless mountain slopes of Nepal. All this mud travels down to the sea and is dumped into the Bay of Bengal. Here an island of mud, covering five million hectares is gradually building up. This is the soil that Nepal should be using for growing crops.

Coal
Coal supplies about one third of the world's energy. It will last another 400 years. Gas supplies about one fifth of the world's energy and will last almost as long as the oil (about thirty years).

Britain's hedgerows
During the 1960s and 1970s, 225,000 kms of hedgerows were destroyed in Great Britain. This removed very valuable nesting and sheltering places for our birds and animals. Hedgerows also act as windbreaks. They help trap soil and stop it from being blown away.

Largest oil-field
The world's largest oil-field is in Saudi Arabia. It covers an area of 8,400 km^2. Oil supplies about one half of the world's energy. The world's oil supplies will be gone in about thirty years' time.

Feeding Egypt
Egypt used to grow all the grain it needed to feed its population. Today it has to bring in 75% of all its food needs from abroad.

Further information

There are many organisations involved with helping nature and our environment. Below are the addresses of just some of the more well known ones that you may like to contact. They may also be able to put you in touch with local organisations, if you want to get actively involved with things such as fund-raising through sponsored events. Remember, our natural world needs every friend and helper it can get!

Friends of the Earth
26-28 Underwood Street
London N1 7JQ

World Wide Fund for Nature
Panda House
Weyside Park
Godalming
Surrey GU7 1XR

British Trust for Nature Conservation Volunteers
36 St Mary's Street
Wallingford
Oxfordshire OX10 0EU

Greenpeace
30-31 Islington Green
London N1 8XT

The Soil Association
86 Colston Street
Bristol BS1 5BB

The Conservation Trust
George Palmer Site
Northumberland Avenue
Reading
Berkshire RG2 7PW

Royal Society for the Protection of Birds
The Lodge
Sandy
Bedfordshire

The People's Trust for Endangered Species
Hamble house
Meadrow
Godalming
Surrey GU7 3JX

Glossary

Carbon dioxide A gas with no taste, colour or smell found in the Earth's air.

Channel A small ditch used to carry water from one place to another.

Chemicals Substances that are in and used by all living things. Organic chemicals come from plants, animals and coal. They can be changed from one form into another through a chemical reaction.

Combine harvester A large farm machine which cuts crops, such as wheat and corn, and separates the grain from the straw.

Decomposers Plants or animals that feed on nature's waste and help to break it down into other forms. In this way important chemicals are returned to the soil and can be re-used.

Dissolve To make or become liquid. Here, it means to disappear or be absorbed.

Dust bowl An area of dry land with no top soil on which nothing can be grown.

Fertilize To use a natural or artificial substance to replace the chemicals taken out of the soil and therefore improve the growth of the plants.

Graze To feed on grass. Cattle and sheep are grazing animals.

Guano The dung of birds, bats and seals used to improve the quality of the soil. Guano is a natural fertilizer.

Hyphae Tiny strands or hairs on the roots of fungi.

Irrigation When water is brought to dry land to make it more suitable for farming.

Lava Hot, liquid rock that has melted because of high temperatures deep inside the Earth. It pours out of volcanoes onto the Earth's surface where it eventually cools and becomes hard.

Microscopic bacteria Tiny living creatures that cannot be seen without a microscope. Some live in the soil or in small lumps, called nodules, on the roots of plants. They can change nitrogen into chemicals which help plants to grow.

Nitrogen gas A gas that makes up most of the Earth's air. Nitrogen is found in all living things and is essential to life.

Organic Something that is natural. Organic farming is natural farming. It uses the waste from plants and animals instead of chemical fertilizer.

Prairies Flat grasslands which are very good for farming because of their rich soil.

Pesticides Man-made chemicals used to kill animals or plants that damage crops.

Terraced A raised, flat space. Steep hillsides can be cut into terraces, or steps, so that the land can be used for farming.

Tropical forests Forests that grow in the hot, rainy parts of the world near the equator. They are also called rainforests. More kinds of plants and animals live in tropical forests than anywhere else on Earth.

Index